HOUSE, HOUSE

HOUSE,

PHOTOGRAPHS BY
THE HOWES BROTHERS
AND JASON STEMPLE

HOUSE

TEXT BY
JANE YOLEN

MARSHALL CAVENDISH   NEW YORK

Marshall Cavendish
99 White Plains Road
Tarrytown, New York 10591

Library of Congress Cataloging-in-Publication Data

Yolen, Jane
House/house / Jane Yolen ; photographs by the Howes brothers and Jason Stemple.
p.   cm.
ISBN 0-7614-5013-0
1. Hatfield (Mass. : Town)—History—Pictorial works. 2. Hatfield (Mass. : Town)—Pictorial works.
3. Hatfield (Mass. : Town)—Social life and customs—Pictorial works. 4. Dwellings—Massachusetts—Hatfield
(Town)—History—Pictorial works 5. Dwellings—Massachusetts—Hatfield (Town)—Pictorial works. I.
Howes brothers (Photographers) II. Stemple, Jason. III. Title.
F74.H45Y65 1998
974.4'23—dc2197-37143
CIP
AC
Book design by Rachel Simon Designs
The text of this book is set in 16 point Windsor
Printed in Italy
First edition
1 3 5 6 4 2

To our Hatfield neighbors

With special thanks to Rita Prew and Robert Sawicki of the Hatfield Historical Society,
and the following who posed in front of their houses, though not all got into the final book:

THE WOODWARD FAMILY
MARSHA HUMPHRIES AND STEPHEN JASINSKI
THE EKUS FAMILY
THE VOLLINGERS
THE BENSON FAMILY
THE KELLOGG FAMILY
CARL PELC
NANCY ASAI AND FREDERICK BARKER
JOAN AND PETER COCKS
BILLY KORZA AND FAMILY
ARTHUR AND ANGELA WRIGHT
THE FOLTS FAMILY
THE BANISTER FAMILY
DAVID STEMPLE

Special thanks to Leeyanne Moore,
who helped me with the research,
and Samuel Pettengill,
who printed the Howes brothers' glass negatives

THE VIEW BUSINESS

FROM 1882-1907 THERE WAS A FAMILY OF PHOTOGRAPHERS—Alvah, Walter, and George Howes—who traveled from place to place in the Connecticut River Valley. They took black-and-white photographs of school classes, factory workers, family groupings, and a series of shots of people in front of their houses. The Howes brothers sold the prints of those pictures to the householders, three for a dollar.

More than twenty thousand of their glass-plate negatives have survived, giving us an amazing visual record of New England at the turn of the century.

The Howes brothers considered themselves in the "view" business. They were not trying to leave a cultural record for the future. They were simply trying to make a living. But along the way they created a treasure of images from a time very different from our own.

One of the towns they visited was Hatfield, a sleepy little farm community in western Massachusetts with a population of fifteen hundred. There, in the early 1900s, they photographed over one hundred houses with the owners standing proudly and stiffly outside, often surrounded by their prize possessions. There are, of course, no telephone or electric lines, no television antennas, no cars in the driveways. It is too soon for such things.

Color photography had not been invented.

A hundred years later, a young Hatfield photographer, Jason Stemple, recreated the Howes pictures.

Most of the homes the brothers had photographed still exist, though many of them are greatly changed. Over they years porches have been removed, new rooms and windows added, clapboards painted, shutters discarded, doorways re-situated, trees planted or cut down. Sometimes an entire house has been moved to a different street.

And now there are power lines and cable lines and phone lines stretching across the photos. There are cars or motorcycles in the driveways or speeding by on the road. The clothing is simpler, freer, less elegant but infinitely more comfortable, especially for women and girls. The population of the town is 3,446.

Stemple's camera captures how the people today own—or are owned—by their houses just as the Howes brothers did a century before.

In color.

Something has been lost—something has been gained.

In 1900, a boy and his dog could ride from Hatfield
to nearby Northampton on an electric trolley,
though heavy winter snows often
closed the trolley lines down. Fifteen
years later, automobiles started
showing up on local streets.
A new car then cost
less than $1,400.

In 1934, buses took the place of trolleys and the trolley
tracks were removed. Many roads began
to be paved. Today there is no public
transportation in or out of Hatfield,
but almost every household has
a car, often several. A new car
costs well over $10,000.

At one time a family's clothes were sewn entirely by hand. It took many hours of labor to make a dress or a pair of pants. Then, in **1846**, the sewing machine was invented. By **1890**, Singer claimed "Ten Million Sewing Machines for family use." By **1900**, local stores were advertising "ready-made" clothing, such as a "Boys Stripe Knee Pants Suite" for **$4.50**; with long pants, **$6.75**.

Today hardly anyone sews clothes by hand. Why
should they, when a trip to the local mall with its
dozens of stores takes only a couple of hours?
An entire family can be dressed for the year
in what is purchased in a single trip. That
clothing is made by machines in great
factories, often in far-away countries
in Asia. An inexpensive boy's suit
now starts at $49.95.

Well into the 1900s, farming was Hatfield's major occupation. Shade-grown tobacco for cigar wrappers was the leading crop. Tobacco warehouses employed many of the townsfolk during winter months. There were also societies dedicated to stamping out "the lamentable influence of tobacco."
They were not very successful.

Today, there are few working tobacco farms left in
the town. Potatoes, cucumbers, asparagus, and berries
are the major crops. Tobacco can be grown more
cheaply in South America. Smoking in America,
at its height in **1965** when **50** percent
of the country indulged, is now down
to **24** percent of the population.

In the early **1800s,** Hatfield girls went to school four
months of the year, because the town would not
vote more money than that for the education
of females. But by **1900,** Hatfield classes
were finally co-ed the entire
school year.

Today children of Hatfield—boys and girls—go to a
school that has computers, a gymnasium, a library,
a PA system, a lunchroom serving hot meals,
and organized after-school sports programs.
None of these things were
in that earlier school.

The first telephones came to western Massachusetts
in 1877, one year after Alexander Graham Bell
received his patent. Within the first five years,
only one hundred phones were installed
in valley homes, very few of them
in Hatfield.

Today, every single house in Hatfield has at least one
telephone; most have jacks for several phones.
And many of the houses have computer
modems and faxes running through
the telephone lines, as well.

In the **1860s**, chewing gum, margarine, typewriters, and can openers were invented. In the **1870s**, the phonograph and ketchup were invented. Tomatoes were considered poisonous until the **1880s**. In the **1890s**, the radio, Tootsie Rolls, Cracker Jacks, cold cereals, and aspirin were invented. In **1904** the first ice cream cone was made. Laborers earned about **$1.60** a day.

In the 1990s, self-adhesive postage stamps, fake fat,
Beanie Babies, and prepackaged salads were invented.
Computer-generated special effects were used in the
movies. The Internet and the worldwide web
became available to all. A mechanical rover
landed on Mars, sending home photographs
and moving pictures that were shown
on television. The minimum
wage was $5.25 an hour.

In the early **1900s**, the average life expectancy in
Hatfield, as in the rest of America, was forty-seven
years, up from thirty-nine in Colonial times.
One of the worst diseases was consumption,
or tuberculosis, also called the "white death."
Children regularly died of diphtheria,
tetanus, whooping cough,
and the flu.

Today, tuberculosis has been practically wiped out due
to a vaccine developed in **1924** and to streptomycin,
developed in **1944.** Babies get shots to keep them
from getting diphtheria, tetanus, whooping cough.
The flu rarely kills anyone. Life expectancy
for men is seventy-plus, women, eighty-plus.
Now people die more often of
heart attacks, cancer, or **AIDS.**

Photographs before **1900** look awkward and stiff,
for people had to stand very still while the
photographer worked his magic. The
pictures were always in black and white.
A brownie camera in **1905** cost a dollar;
the six-exposure film cost fifteen cents.

Today, Polaroid cameras can produce a finished color picture in a minute. People can even move about while a photo is being shot. The color photographs in this book were made using a Nikon F4. The body of the camera cost **$1,800**, the lens **$500**. Each 36-exposure film cost **$10**.

In **1890**, a housewife might wait a long time till the grocery wagon came by. The horse-drawn wagon was used for delivering meat, bread, milk, butter, cheese— almost all from local farmers. She stored those things in an ice box, where they were kept cold by the use of ice. The first household refrigerator was not built until **1913**. The housewife knew the grocer and driver by name.

Today, a trip by car to a supermarket takes only a few
minutes. Distances may be farther, but the choices
are greater: oranges from Israel, cheese from
Holland, rice from India, Australian beef.
These can be kept fresh in a refrigerator
or freezer, cooked on a gas or electric
stove, reheated in a microwave.
The customer will not know the
supermarket owner's name.

In **1898**
Sugar: **4** cents a pound.
Butter: **25** cents a pound.
Hamburger on toast sandwich: **7** cents.
A ride to the next town took well over an hour.

In 1998

Sugar: **$2.00** a five-pound bag, or **40** cents a pound.
Butter: **$2.19** a pound.
Hamburger on a bun at McDonalds: **69** cents.
A ride to the next town takes eight minutes by car.

An **1893** bike advertisement with a black-and-white
drawing of an oversized three-wheeler:
"Cripples, ladies and girls, if you want air
or exercise, buy a Fairy Tricycle, foot
or hand p'w'r, CHEAP FOR ALL."

Today a bike advertisement shows a color photo of
a woman on a red racing bike:
"THE COMPETITION IS SEEING RED.
Susan DeMattei 1996 Atlanta
Olympics Bronze Medal Winner."

In 1906, when this picture was taken, a maid lived in
the attic, in a little room with bright yellow-flowered
wallpaper. The room was freezing in the winter
and sweltering in the summer. To go to the toilet,
she used an indoor three-hole privy on the
first floor, as did the rest of the household.
She did all the work in the house
from sunup to sundown.

Today, the writer of this book works in the same little
attic room. The flowered wallpaper is now faded
and brown. There is an air conditioner to keep
the room cool in summer and electric baseboard
heat to keep it warm in winter. There are three
full bathrooms—two on the first floor, one
on the second. The author works at her
writing from sunup to sundown.

Historical Capawonk. Hatfield Historical Society, Hatfield, Massachusetts, 1970.

Historic Hampshire in the Connecticut Valley, by Clifton Johnson.
Milton Bradley Company. Springfield, Massachusetts/Northampton Historical Society, Northampton, Massachusetts, 1932.

Images of America: Northampton, by James M. Parsons. Arcadia Publishing, Dover, New Hampshire, 1996.

The Look of Paradise, by Jacqueline Van Voris. Northampton Historical Society, Northampton, Massachusetts, 1984.

Meadow City Milestones by Alice H. Manning. Daily Hampshire Gazette, Northampton, Massachusetts.

New England Refelections 1882-1907, by Alan B. Newman. Pantheon Books, New York, 1981.

Pictureseque Hampshire, A Supplement to the Quarter-Centennial Journal, 1890.

Pioneer Valley: A Pictorial History, by Guy A. McLain. The Donning Company, Virginia Beach, Virginia, 1991.

Say Goodbye to the Valley, by Wes Patience. Connecticut Valley Historical Museum/Springfield Library and Museums Association, Springfield, Massachusetts, 1994.

St. Nicholas Reader for Young Folks, edited by Mary Mapes Dodge. August 1983, May 1983. The Century Union Company, 1983.

Tales of Amherst, A Look Back, by Daniel Lombardo. The Jones Library, Inc., Amherst, Massachusetts, 1986.

The Writer's Guide to Everyday Life in the 1800s, by Marc McCutcheon. Writer's Digest Books, Cincinnatti, Ohio, 1992.